WISE OLE OWL

The Language of HeavenEase

Dedication

As in the days of old,
there was a firstfruit we are told
Entering into covenant with THE KING
This Firstfruit to HIM I bring
MY thanks and Praise and ALL the Glory
As HE helps ME to tell the Old Old story.

WISE OLE OWL
The Language of HeavenEase

Written by Marcella O'Banion Burnes
Illustrated by Aaron Jones

BOLD TRUTH PUBLISHING

Christian Literature and Artwork
A BOLD TRUTH Publication

WISE OLE OWL
Copyright © 2017 Marcella Burnes

ISBN 10: 0-9991469-2-0
ISBN 13: 978-0-9991469-2-7

FIRST EDITION

Marcella Burnes
P.O. Box 127
North Miami, Oklahoma 74358
marcellaburnes@yahoo.com

BOLD TRUTH PUBLISHING
(Christian Literature & Artwork)
606 West 41st, Ste. 4
Sand Springs, Oklahoma 74063
www.BoldTruthPublishing.com

Available from Amazon.com and other retail outlets.
Orders by U.S. trade bookstores and wholesalers.
Email beirep@yahoo.com

Quantity sales special discounts are available on quantity
purchases by corporations, associations, and others. For
details, contact the publisher at the address above.

Artwork & Design by Aaron Jones www.wildartbyaaron.com

Printed in the USA.
08 17   10 9 8 7 6 5 4 3 2 1

Special Acknowledgements

To my Aunt Berneice,
For from her hand she does release
a Blessing from above.
I ACKNOWLEDGE HER WITH GREAT LOVE.

To Rebecca Lou and Jarrod too!
Without you what would I do?
A listening ear, an encouraging cheer,
for pushing me forward when quitting was so near!

To Charlie and Wanda
For prayers for my soul,
for Understanding how far I had to go.
Never judgement, just love,
directly from HIM above.

To Jug and Brenda
Thank you for the Bed and Bread,
for I was always well fed!!!

To Public Library in my Hometown
All eyes saw me coming,
but they never frowned.

WISE OLE OWL

A wise ole owl once said to me
"Are you prepared for Eternity?"
"Why yes, I am" said I to he,
"What makes you ask?
Are you also free?"

"Do you know JESUS?
Does HE know you?
Do you speak the language
of HeavenEase?"

"HeavenEase?"
Said he to me
Blinking rather sleepily.

3

"What is this?
Some kind of dis-ease?"

"OH NO!" said I to he
"Absolutely no disease
Why HeavenEase helped set me free
It's the language of Eternity."

"I've never heard of such a thing," he declared
"Is it something new, in the air?"

"OH NO! Not new at all
Ancient of Days did let it fall
It's common knowledge 'round all our folk'
We take it not lightly, and we don't joke,
bout this language that we need.
It helps us on our way to eternity."

"WAY to Eternity?" questioned he of me
"It be not THE WAY, for that is HE
The WONDROUS SAVIOUR,
JESUS HE BE," said I to he.

4

"But the language of HeavenEase
Brings us to that place on our knees
Where we speak and it flows like a breeze.
It takes us to the battleground
Where Heaven's battles are ragin' round.
It brings us safely through these."

"And this is fought on your knees?"
posed he to me.
"This seems such an impossiblity.
But tell me more, would you please?"

"I'll tell you more, certainly,
But I thought you a wise ole owl to be?
I thought you would know HeavenEase."

"Ohhh, I'm wise.
But my eyes
were blinded by the enemy
When I was only three.
He told me I was a joke,
At my spiritual eyes he took a poke."

"Oh my goodness," said I to he.
"You seemed ok, to me."

"Yeah I know," said he to me,
"Most folks think that I can see.
But tell me more, tell me please,
Of this language of HeavenEase."

"Well," said I, "Acts 19:2 says to me,
Have ye received the HOLY GHOST
Since you believed?
We have not heard of such a thing.
These are words of those who dream.
___ Words spoken of old
From the Apostle Paul, we're told."

"Now I've heard those words
In the Wise Ole BOOK.
I AM AN OWL
I've took a look.

These things have passed away.
These are not for owls these days."

"Oh my goodness," says I to he,
"You've GOT to be kidding me!
When you took a look in the Book
Did you not see the room HE shook?"
"The Mercy of the HOLY ONE
Was given through HIS ONLY SON
When HIS work on Earth was done
HE said a Comforter would come."

"IN THAT HOUR
HE came with GREAT POWER.
A MIGHTY rushing wind was HE,
With cloven tongues of fire to receive.
HE sat upon Believers that day
And HE has NEVER, NEVER gone away."

11

"First Corinthians 14:2
Will prove this is true.
And so a language, a Heavenly Gift,
An open flow to help heal a rift,
Between the ONE and ONLY GOD
And the Sons of Men
Who on this Earth do trod."

"When in this language we do speak
a HEAVENLY VOICE
Can make us weep.
"It gives us power
TO STRENGTHEN our 'inner man'
And pray the prayers of GOD'S command."

12

"But this was done in olden day,
and in this language we no longer pray.
Prove to me, if you please,
How this could still be?"

"First Corinthians the 14th Chapter
Is the teaching you are after.
Every thought of this Chapter
Tells us HeavenEase,
Is the language we should desire after."

"Also, the book of Jude 1:20
Speaks of this clear and plenty."

"Besides," said I to he,
"If you're as wise as you claim to be?
And said you've looked in the Book...
OHHH, but WAIT!!!
You said you've been blind since three,
It's no wonder, you can't REALLY SEE."

7 But, beloved, remember ye the words which were spoken before of the apostles of our Lord Jesus Christ;

18 How that they told you there should be mockers in the last time, who should walk after their own ungodly lusts.

19 These be they who separate themselves, sensual, having not the Spirit.

20 But ye, beloved, building up yourselves on your most holy faith, praying in the Holy Ghost,

21 Keep yourselves in the love of God, looking for the mercy of our Lord Jesus Christ unto eternal life.

22 And of some have compassion, making difference:

23 And others save with fear, pulling them out of the fire; hating even the garment spotted by the flesh.

24 Now unto him that is able to keep you from falling, and to present you faultless before the presence of his glory with exceeding joy, the only wise God our Saviour

"For the language of HeavenEase
Comes from faith of those who see.
FAITH cometh by hearing we are told,
So on the GOSPEL you must be sold."

"This GOSPEL I know," said he to me
"The FATHER, The SON,
The HOLY GHOST.
These three I love the most."

"For I saw these when I had my sight,
Before I was blinded with this terrible plight.
But this language gives me a fright,
It makes me want to take flight."

"But that's because you cannot see."
The Wise Ole Book says to me,
"Lack of knowledge will destroy thee.
HOSEA 4:6 is where this is found,
If you care to hear I will expound."

"Yes," said he,
"Expound to me."

"That's what happened to your eyes.
The ole crafty enemy blinded you with lies.
JOHN 10:10 will set you free.
Expose the liar and give sight to thee."

"I...I...I...beg your pardon,"
He stammered with great surprise,
"DID YOU SAY SIGHT TO MY EYES?"

"Of course, just hear and believe.
'Cause every way I read,
The Wise Ole Book,
I just Believe,
When I take a look."

"I do believe," says he to me,
"And now I'm really beginning to see.
I just needed those things pointed out to me."

"Heavenly things come from above
They are sent to us in HIS LOVE
But we must receive those things HE sends,
Especially this language
that blows on HIS wind."

"WHOOO!"
Said the wise ole owl
That once was blind,
But now could see,
As he flew away to the trees.

"WHOOO,
Do they say is
I AM?
THE ALPHA
THE OMEGA
THE BEGINNING AND
THE END!!!"

Enjoy these other great books from
Bold Truth Publishing

Seemed Good to
THE HOLY GHOST
by Daryl P Holloman

EFFECTIVE PRISON Ministries
by Wayne W. Sanders

How to Overcome Stormy Weather
by Wayne W. Sanders

Obedience is Not an Option
by Brian Ohse

TURN OFF THE STEW
by Judy Spencer

KINGDOM of LIGHT 1 - kingdom of darkness
Truth about Spiritual Warfare
by Michael R. Hicks

The Holy Spirit SPEAKS Expressly
by Elizabeth Pruitt Sloan

Matthew 4:4
Man shall not live by bread alone,
but by every word that proceedeth out of the mouth of God.
by Rick McKnight

THE BLOOD COVENANT
by Ronnie Moore

Supernatural Guidance
by Ronnie Moore

C.H.P. - Coffee Has Priority
The Memoirs of a California Highway Patrol Officer - Badge 9045
by Ed Marr

PITIFUL or POWERFUL
THE CHOICE IS YOURS
by Rachel V. Jeffries

VICTIM TO VICTOR
THE CHOICE IS YOURS
by Rachel V. Jeffries

I Have a Story to Tell
...out of his belly shall flow rivers of living water. - John 7:38
by Jean Carlburg

THE GIFT of KNOWING Our Heavenly Father
Abiding in Intimacy
by Deborah K. Reed

SEEING BEYOND
...out of his belly shall flow rivers of living water. - John 7:38
by Kelly Taylor Nutt

SPIRITUAL BIRTHING
Bringing God's Plans & Purposes and Manifestation
by Lynn Whitlock Jones

BECOMING PERFECT
Let The Perfector Perfect His Work In You
by Sally Stokes Weiesnbach

In the SECRET PLACE of the MOST HIGH
God's Word for Supernatural Healing, Deliverance & Protection
by Aaron Jones

FIVE SMOOTH STONES
by Aaron Jones

Available at Select Bookstores and at
www.BoldTruthPublishing.com

Experience all the JOY, LOVE and WONDER as your children discover JESUS CHRIST the MIRACLE-WORKER through The Adventures of these 2 unlikely friends.

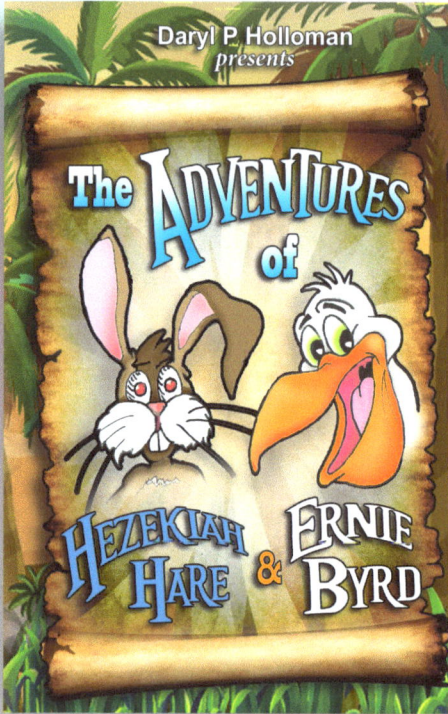

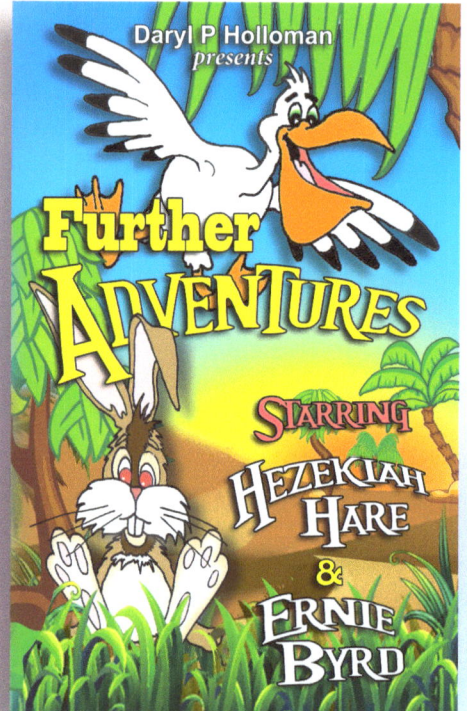

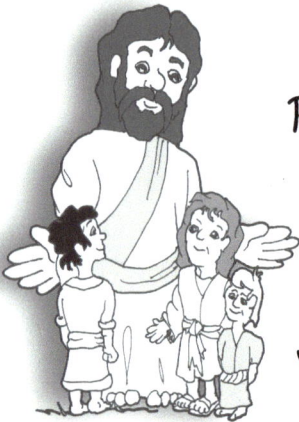

Written by
Prophet and Missionary Daryl P Holloman
(with over 100 Pen & Ink Illustrations)
These books are sure to become
CHILDEN'S BOOK CLASSICS.
A must have in any Faith Library.
YOU'VE NEVER HEARD THE GOSPEL
STORY TOLD LIKE THIS!